How to Write a Research Proposal and a Thesis: *A Manual for Students and Researchers*

2nd Edition

How to Write a Research Proposal and a Thesis: *A Manual for Students and Researchers*

Second Edition

Mohamed E. Hamid

6" x 9" (15.24 x 22.86 cm)

Black & White on White paper, 62 pages

ISBN-13: 978-1482675054; ISBN-10: 1482675056

Printed By:

CreateSpace: A DBA of On-Demand Publishing LLC, part of the Amazon group of companies

First edition (2010).

Where observation is concerned chance favors only the prepared mind"

L. PASTEUR (1900)

"It has been noted that a one-year registered postgraduate student often fails to provide readily his/ her objectives in term of to do, to perform, to develop or to study... Etc"

THE AUTHOR OF THIS BOOK (2001)

TABLE OF CONTENTS

PREFACE TO THE SECOND EDITION

This book is intended for students planning to do postgraduate studies, researchers and undergraduate students requested to write down graduation projects. The book follows a simplified approach that beginners can use to preparing proposal (مقترح) and writing theses or dissertations (أطروحة / فرضية). It describes meaning, stages and methods of writing a successful research project proposal and a thesis from the first draft proposal to the final version of the thesis. Many terminologies and technical terms have been translated into Arabic.

In this edition as in the previous one, a significant part is devoted to the proposal. A good written proposal often leads to a successful thesis and dissertation. A definition was given to terms such as hypothesis (فرضية), theory (نظرية) and research (بحث). Readers may go first to how to write a thesis section or any part of it, but chronological reading of the book will ensure maximum benefits. It has been noted that a one-year registered postgraduate student may fail to state at once his/ her objectives in term of: to do, to perform, to develop or to study... Etc. That is, in a brief and meaningfully way. In addition, students mix up between literature review and discussion, as frequently there are repetitions of sections from introduction or literature review in the discussion chapter, which should be. Discussion is a chapter in which the writer can express his/ her ideas or criticize others works based on his/ her findings and not on any other ground. Important findings in the result chapter should appear in abstract, but these findings may not necessarily constitute the final message or the impact (the conclusion). Some materials or long tables, figures and results may be transferred to the Appendix rather than wasting the readers (or examiner's) valuable time wondering between excessive details in the main pages of the thesis. We noticed that a considerable number of finished theses at many higher academic institutions, but it are noticed that the writing-up did not stick to an organized and scientific standard.

I am grateful to colleagues and students for their encouraging feedback and advice. These have prompted the continuous amendment and improvement. Recommended further readings on the subject are provided at the end of the book to see for variations between different institutions.

Mohamed E. Hamid *(BVSc, MSc, PhD, Fellow AvH)*
Department of Microbiology, College of Medicine, King Khalid University
Abha, KSA.

mehamid2@yahoo.com

Section 1: **OVERVIEW AND DEFINITIONS**

The Proposal and Thesis: An Overview

1.	Think of a title (a problem) What is my tentative title (thesis title)? Why do I want to do this title? Do I need special permission? Will the project involve other people than me? What actually goes (will go) on when I start. (imagine!)?	First draft proposal*
2.	Write a proposal (Research Plan) from your First Draft. With help of supervisor write (fill) in these subtitles: provisional Title, Introduction (with the aims), the Problem (hypothesis, Research questions), Review of literature, Research design, Bibliography (references), Appendix, Re-write first draft until accepted by committee.	The proposal (Research plan)
3.	Investigate the identified problem Describe the mechanism of conducting your research, the data needed to answer your research questions and details of how this will be achieved in practice, it includes: Setting, Sampling procedure, Equipments, Methods of study, Statistical analysis etc.	Design & Methodology
4.	Data collection and analysis Record and analyze data, with or without graphics, tables... Etc	Results (Data collection)
5.	Criticize, relate ad argue your recorded data and results.	Discussion
6.	Give conclusions, recommendations and implications of your findings to others.	Conclusions
7.	Write and arrange thesis into chapters: Title page, Summary, Introduction, Literature Review, Methods, Results, Discussion, Conclusions, References and Appendix.	Writing up
8.	It is essential that Thesis writer checks (proof read) his/her text for common errors e.g. punctuations, omissions, spellings, agreement, singular/ plural, headings, verbs...	Proofreading
9.	One of the requirements for certain advanced degrees is an oral examination or a presentation by the student where he/she is questioned by examiners, committee or jury and audience.	Thesis defense (viva voce)
10.	The student submits a complete copy of the thesis to institution, along with the appropriate completed forms.	Submission

Candidate is advised to takes steps one after another to achieve his/ her objectives.

DEFINITIONS

PROPOSAL (مقترح)

A proposal is a written plan for a thesis/ dissertation or other scientific projects, which is developed by a student for consideration and approval by relevant committees (see SECTION 2 for more details).

THESIS (أطروحة / رسالة)

A thesis (pl. theses) or a dissertation is a document submitted in support of candidature (applicant) for a degree or professional qualification presenting the author's research and findings (ISO, 1986) (see SECTION 3 for more details). In some countries/ universities, the word thesis is used as part of a bachelor's or master's course, while dissertation is normally applied to a doctorate.

HYPOTHESIS (فرضية)

A hypothesis is a tentative statement that proposes a possible explanation to some phenomenon (E.g. Ultra violet light may cause skin cancer) or event or idea that can be experimentally tested with the lowest level of confidence (see SECTION 2 for more details).

RESEARCH (بحث)

Research means systematic investigation (تحقيق) and study of materials and sources using scientific methods in order to establish facts and reach new conclusions. The ultimate aim of research is to contribute in some way to the existing knowledge we have in particular field.

Research is the major way for producing theses and dissertations and books or other forms of published works. To the average person research, probably means finding out something he or she did not previously know. A researcher needs to finding out a firm answer to question that he or she may know already.

Traditionally, research has been classified into:

a) Primary: which deals with the main source of information E.g.: The influence of adding calcium to the diet of chicken on egg production
b) Secondary: which concentrates on available data (books, other forms of published literature) on increasing egg production

THEORY (نظرية)

A theory, in the scientific sense of the word, is an analytic structure designed to explain a set of empirical observations. A scientific theory does two things:

1. Identifies a set of distinct observations as a class of phenomena
2. Makes statement about the underlying reality that brings about or affects this class

In the scientific or empirical tradition, the term "theory" is reserved for ideas, which meet baseline requirements about the kinds of empirical observations made, the methods of classification used, and the consistency of the theory in its application among members of the class to which it pertains. These requirements vary across different scientific fields of knowledge. In general, theories are expected to be functional and economical: i.e. a theory should be the simplest possible tool that can be used effectively to address the given class of phenomena.

LITERATURE REVIEW (استعراض الأدب أو المطبوعات)

A literature review is a summary of previous research on a topic. Literature reviews can be either a part of a larger report of a research project, a thesis or a bibliographic essay that is published separately in a scholarly journal (http://www.library.ncat.edu/ref/guides/literaturereview).

A literature review is a body of text (written via paraphrasing or quotation) that aims to assess the critical points of current knowledge and or methodological approaches on a particular topic. Literature reviews are secondary sources, and as such, does not report any new or original experimental work (Hart, 2001).

REFERENCES (BIBLIOGRAPHY; المراجع)

A reference (مرجع), in academic literature, is a previously published written work within academic publishing that has been used as a source for theory or claims referred to in the text. References contain complete bibliographic information so the interested reader can find them (in libraries). References can be added either at the end of the publication or as footnotes (حاشية).

Bibliography (قائمة المراجع) is a systematic list of books and other works such as journal articles. Bibliographies range from "works cited" lists at the end of books and articles to complete, independent publications.

Formats in citing references (bibliography) vary, but an entry for a book or other sources usually contains the following information: author(s), title, publisher, volume, pages and date of publication

DIFFERENCE BETWEEN MASTER AND DOCTORATE THESES

Stuart (1979) stated the following to distinguish between the master and doctorate level:

1. A master thesis must demonstrate the candidate's ability to make use of an appropriate research procedure, to organize primary and secondary information into a meaningful whole and to present the results in acceptable writing (prose). The length the thesis is not important as long as these aims are fulfilled.
2. A doctoral dissertation is expected to represent independent and original research in the field of candidate's graduate study. It must add, in some way, to the understanding in the candidate's field. Such contribution to knowledge may result either from the critical examination of materials not hitherto dealt with or from the re examination of traditional materials by means of new techniques or from new points of view. The project undertaken must be of sufficiently difficult and scope to test the candidate's ability to carry on further research of his/her own and it must ensure that the candidate masters the skills needed for such research.

Mauch and Birch (1990) defined the thesis as the product of scholarly (علمية) and professional (مهنية) study at the master degree level by a graduate student. It is usually a document in a format and style specified by a particular academic institution.

Sometimes a thesis is regarded as synonymous with dissertation, that can be acceptable, nevertheless Mauch and Birch (1990) linked theses with

(11)

master degrees and dissertation with doctorate degrees. According to these authors, the level, which distinguishes a dissertation from other studies, is essentially by its deeper, more comprehensive and more mature professional and scholarly treatment of the subject.

Theses and dissertations differ from books in that a book is literally a written or printed work consists of pages bounded in a cover, which is intended for publication rather than for a degree as the case with theses or dissertations. Thesis can be published after that as a book. Accordingly, it is called published thesis contrary to the unpublished thesis.

At this stage, we need to define the proposal that happens before a thesis or a dissertation . A proposal (suggestion, الاقتراح) is a written plan for a thesis or for a dissertation, which developed by a student for consideration and approval by relevant committees.

Section 2: **PROPOSAL**

THE FIRST DRAFT PROPOSAL

Before you write the first draft, think of these two questions:

1. **WHAT** is my tentative title (thesis title)? E.g.: i) Development of advanced life support system; ii) Subsurface filtration pilot plant in elimination of nitrogen and phosphorous pollution from lake water; iii) Xanthan fermentation of mixed potato waste, iv) Evaluation of HINI vaccine in protecting children in X and Y region etc...
2. **WHY** do I want to do this title? Develop ..., produce ..., evaluate ..., treat ...., analyze, find ....etc.

Answer to WHAT and WHY questions (theoretical justification) is needed, then you proceed to the next questions:

What steps and facilities will I need to accomplish or to help me accomplishing my title?

   - Do I need special permission?
   - Will the project involve other people than me?
   - What actually goes (will go) on when I start, (imagine!)?

Answers to the above six questions will constitute your first draft. Come later and re-read it, make your amendments and clarify it. Take the time to type what you have drafted, with double space, wide margins; make efforts to minimize errors in your statement as this first draft make an impression on your advisor that may last. Make at least three copies: one for your advisor, one for your file and one for you to work with. A formal beginning by the student allows your advisor to help you.

This is a crucial first step in establishing a positive student- supervisor relationship. Such discipline will help you establish and keep your records. At this point, "an ounce of order is worth a pound of clutter".

DETAILED RESEARCH PROPOSAL (PLAN)

Research proposal (plan) is what you propose to do. It shows that you understand your field of research and you know how to conduct that research. Some advisors recommend the proposal to be short of two to three pages to be handed to the committee for approval. Other preferred a detailed research plan. Although no one format is common among higher academic institutions, a research proposal usually consists of the following elements:

Candidates can write either:

1. A short research proposal
2. A long research proposal

SHORT RESEARCH PROPOSAL

A short research proposal typically includes the following sections:

1. Title page
2. Introduction
3. Objectives
4. Literature Review
5. Design and methodology
6. Bibliography (References)

LONG RESEARCH PROPOSAL

A long research proposal may contain many titles and subtitles namely:

1. Title page
2. Introduction
3. Objectives (*or Introduction and Objective as one unit*)
4. Literature Review
5. Design, methodology and procedures (*protocol*)
6. Ethical considerations (*where applicable*)
7. Time schedule
8. Delineations and limitations of proposal
9. Budget (*where applicable*)
10. Bibliography (References)
11. Appendix

DETAILS OF PROPOSAL SECTIONS

Now, 1 detail all sections including those in the short or the long research proposal:

Title page

It includes:

- Title
- Name, qualifications and address of candidate
- Name, qualifications and address of advisors/ supervisors
- Place of experiments
- Duration
- The title

The title should:

- Be informative and concise
- Convey to the reader the main focus of your research

Try to limit your title to a single sentence and exclude any words that are not essential to the overall understanding of the title.

The title is usually only formulated after the research problems have been stated in a final format. The wording of the title can be altered at a later stage of the research when necessary; this is why the word "provisional" has been kept. Examples:

- Bioactive substances from bacteria isolated from the mangroves of Saudi Arabia
- The effect of kaolin on enrichment of denitrifiers; preliminary assessment of air quality in ...
- The presence and absence of calcium chloride on growth of bakery yeast *Saccharomyces cerevisiae*

INTRODUCTION

The purpose of this section is to provide a background for the material to follow and to set up the hypothesis.

The following elements are usually discussed in the introduction:

1. Statement of the problem (theme)
2. Research question (s)
3. Hypothesis
4. Significant and research outcomes
5. Statement of the problem (theme)

Statement of the problem (theme)

Research forms a circle, it starts with a problem and ends with a solution to the problem. This is a summary of research theme, aims and objectives and it indicates the originality of your research or gabs-, which- your research will fill. The statement gives direction to the study; it gives information about the scope and suggests how the study will be done. The statement, after all, must be clear concise and unambiguous. The research problem should be stated in such a way that it would lead to analytical thinking on the research with the aim of possibly finding a concluding solution to the stated problem.

Examples:

"This thesis deals with cotton marketing and manufacturing in the Sudan (Zulfo, 1981).

"This study concerns with the prevention of drug misuse among secondary school students in Khartoum state (El Hilo, 1992)".

The purpose of this study is to investigate creativity among children in selected school in Khartoum state with emphasis on the use of drawing as an indicator.

The increase use of organochlorine insecticide in the irrigated schemes dictates the importance of investigating the hazardous effects of these compounds on human and animal. This study is an attempt to detect organochlorine residues in samples from farmers and to correlate the presence of these residues with the occurrence of the lung cancer among farmer.

Elements (below in bold) and objectives (to ...) extracted from the above statement can be written as direct objective as follows:

1. To detect **residues** of organochlorine insecticide in farmers samples
2. To record clinical and **pathological findings** in the tested farmers
3. To **correlate** between the level of organochlorine compounds in farmers samples and the recorded clinical signs

Research questions:

Examples of research questions taken from the above are:

1. Why there are more lung cancer cases among farmers than other sectors of the community?

2. Is there any relation between the level of organochlorine compounds in farmer's samples and the occurrence of lung cancer among farmers?

Hypothesis:

To turn a research question: why there is more lung cancer among farmers than other sectors of the community? Into hypothesis is as follows: "frequent application of the organochlorine insecticide in farms resulted in the development of lung cancer among farmers".

A hypothesis is a tentative statement that proposes a possible explanation to some phenomenon (E.g. Ultra violet light may cause skin cancer) or event or idea that can be experimentally tested with the lowest level of confidence (null hypothesis).

Investigators often develop a hypothesis that helps give direction to their work. Hypothesis can be developed from reviewing the literature because it needs knowledge. Therefore, an hypothesis is a supposition, proposition or unproved theory tentatively advanced to explain observed facts or phenomenon, or a proposition made as basis for reasoning without the a assumption of truth.

Three questions will help constructing a hypothesis:

1. **Validly** (ساري المفعول، شرعي): are there good reasons, practical experience, and theories on previous research findings that tend to support it? If yes, it can be said that the hypothesis have been constructed validly
2. **Testability** (خاضعة للاختبار): is it possible to collect and analyze data in such a way as to show whether the hypothesis stands up? If so, the hypothesis is testable
3. **Relevance** (وثاقة الصلة بالموضوع): does the hypothesis focus on the problem under study? To be relevant, a hypothesis must answer part or all of the matter being investigated

Example:

"Ultra violet light may cause skin cancer" this can be formalized as follows: "if skin cancer is related to ultraviolet light, then people with a high exposure to UV light will have a higher frequency of skin cancer"

Formalized hypotheses contain two variables:

1. Independent: The independent variables are the ones you, the "scientist" control E.g.: Ultra violet

1. Dependent: The dependent variables are the ones that you observe and/or measure the results E.g.: skin cancer

Plant growth may be affected by the color of the light" this can be formalized as follows: "if leaf color change is related to light, then exposing plants to various wavelengths of light will result in changes in leaf color..

The failure of pregnancy in sheep in the Takyo region is due to the high temperature". This hypothesis was constructed because the student has some knowledge. Examples of his knowledge or facts:

- Female sheep (ewes) mate every 16 to 17 days during the breeding season till they become pregnant
- Farmer identify the pregnant ewes by the fact that they don't mate further
- Many ewes appear pregnant but they produce no lambs
- High temperature is known to affect embryo survival in other species

After a hypothesis has been repeatedly tested, a hierarchy of scientific thoughts develops. Hypothesis is the most common, with the lowest level of certainty. A theory is a hypothesis that has been repeatedly tested with little modification, e.g. the theory of evolution. A law is one of the fundamental underlying principles of how the universe is organized, e.g. the laws of thermodynamics, Newton's law of gravity. Science uses the word theory differently than it is used in the general population. Theory to most people, in general non-scientific use, is an untested idea. Scientists call this a hypothesis.

Technically, each hypothesis should be stated using:

1. Null (H0) and
2. Alternative hypotheses (H1)

Example:

Suppose you conducted a drug trial on a group of animals and you hypothesized that the animals receiving the drug would show increased heart rates compared to those that did not receive the drug. You conduct the study and collect the following data:

- H0: The proportion of animals whose heart rate increased is independent of drug treatment.
- H1: The proportion of animals whose heart rate increased is associated with drug treatment

The results:

	Heart Rate Increased	No Heart Rate Increase	Total
Treated	36	14	50
Not treated	30	25	55
Total	66	39	105

- H0: The proportion of animals whose heart rate increased is independent of drug treatment
- H1: The proportion of animals whose heart rate increased is associated with drug treatment

Test of independence between the rows and columns (Chi-square):

Chi-square (Observed value)	3.418
Chi-square (Critical value)	9.488
DF	4
p-value	0.491
Alpha	0.05

Test interpretation:

- H0: The rows and the columns of the table are independent.
- H1: There is a link between the rows and the columns of the table.
- P-value is greater than the significance level alpha=0.05, one cannot reject the null hypothesis H0. The risk to reject the null hypothesis H0 while it is true is 49.05%.

Significance and research outcomes

The researcher should indicate and defend why it is necessary to undertake the research. The benefits that will result from the research and to whom it will be beneficial should be indicated. You need to communicate enthusiasm and confidence for the research, arguing clearly as to the contribution it will make to the subject area and discipline in general the significance of the study is another way of starting the aims of the study.

Examples:

- Early targeted prevention programs in drug use among people can reduce long-term costs in the general medical sector. It also enhances the overall efficiency of health care service delivery.

- Participation (objectively) in deterring and eradication of drug misuse emphasizes prevention of problems that affect security of society such as cultivation of Hashish.
- The study calls for further research.
- The study provides a comprehensive analysis.
- There is wide availability and cultivation of Hashish; therefore, there is need for highlighting the fact of the availability.
- There is a fact that secondary school students "misuse drugs": a fact from current knowledge and hence, it states the need for something to be done.

OBJECTIVES

1. General objectives
2. Measurable (specific) objectives

General objectives

You can shape the general objective in a statement as follows:

The objective of this study is to assess the nature and extent of drug misuse among secondary school in Khartoum province and to provide information, which might help in preventing drug misuse among secondary school students in the province.

Measurable (specific) objectives

Examples:

1. To acquire knowledge about drug to understand its devastating effect, its lows and legislations
2. To stimulate more negative attitude towards drug use
3. To develop a sense of moral and values to raise the level of their self-respect (self-esteem)
4. To improve their decision making skill and enable them to avoid the misuse of drug

Meaning of literature

The literature refers to the previous works or sources of information relevant to your research area, either theoretical (idea-based) or empirical (collected or observed data) collected from either i) primary sources ii) secondary sources or iii) tertiary sources.

The literature review for a research proposal may be specific to the development of your proposal. The literature review for proposal does not differ from that written for the thesis, only that in the thesis, more details are given and student expected to survey almost all information published and relevant on his/ her subject.

Purpose of Literature

Literature review tries to:

1. Demonstrate what is known about the subject
2. Indicate the gaps your research
3. Note the original contribution by others
4. Outline some of the limitations and/or gaps in the literature
5. Consider areas for further study that have been identified by other researchers and you may want to consider!
6. Consider where the literature is mainly coming from? Which countries? Areas that could be considered?
7. Identify what are the significant research personalities (institutes) in this area?
8. Identify whether there is a consensus about the topic?
9. Identify aspects that have generated a significant debate on the topic?
10. Identify what methods or problems that have been picked up by others in the field? In addition, how they might affect your research?
11. Indicate what is the most appropriate methodology for your research based on the literature you have reviewed?
12. Indicate what is the status of research in this area?
13. Identify what sources of information or data which have been identified that and might be useful to you?
14. Justify your own research: you need to draw on your literature review to justify your own research (make it sense OK)
15. Interpret the research findings in a better way, determine the relevancy of the prospective research

How to carry out a literature search?

1. Developing a search strategy.
2. Defining the topic - in order to begin your literature review you must first define your research question. What is the purpose? What does it mean? What are the key words? Are there other words, which could be used, such as synonyms, variations in spelling? What do you already know about the topic? What is the scope? Do you need everything ever written in English on this topic, or just the last ten years?
3. Before beginning a search for information, compile a list of keywords. It is important to develop a search strategy that will effectively locate useful and relevant information. This will often involve breaking down an essay or research question into:
4. Keywords or phrases; entering your search; and evaluating your results to determine whether you need to employ various strategies to broaden, narrow or otherwise modify your research
5. Analyzing the topic of an essay question or research topic usually involves making a list of keywords or phrases. You will need to include all the key concepts or ideas contained within the essay or research question. It might be useful to include alternative ways of phrasing and expressing concepts and ideas. Think about both general terms and very specific terms for broadening and narrowing your search. The keyword or phrase is the basic unit of any search. You may find it helpful to consult subject dictionaries and encyclopedias, or a textbook glossary for the common terminology of the subject area. The use of an index and/or thesaurus is also advisable to establish the useful terms
6. Identifying resources - information is available in a number of formats (sources). It is important for you to understand the significance of various formats so that you know what will best suit your information requirements.

Sources of literature

The following are the common sources:

1. Books
2. Reference materials
3. Journals
4. Conference papers
5. Dissertations
6. Internet indexes/abstracts printed
7. Electronic databases
8. Government publications
9. Theses

Reporting verbs

The past simple and present perfect tenses are the most common reporting verbs used in reviewing the literature. Present tense is also used with acceptable facts. When the author is the subject of the reporting verb, use the past simple tense. E.g.:

Ali found that .... Musa noted that ......

Use the present perfect when the subject is hidden and there is no mentioning of a particular experiment. E.g.:

Mycobacterium species has been found to contain mycolic acids in their cell wall (Asselineau et al, 1962).

POWERFUL REPORTING VERBS

E.g.: Report, document, record, certify, confirm, attest, show, prove, proof, verify, found, establish, start, set up, originate, initiate, institute, create.

LESS POWERFUL REPORTING VERBS:

E.g.: Notice, sees, perceives, discerns, observed, said, mentioned, cite, conceal, talk about, state, declare, reveal, and refer.

ARGUABLE REPORTING VERBS:

E.g.: Claim, allege, maintain, assert that, argued that, discuss that...etc.

FACTIVE AND NON-FACTIVE VERBS:

The reporting verbs are divided into factive and non-factive verbs. A verb that asserts the truth of a following clause is a factive verb E.g.:

I know that you were overcharged

I regret that you were overcharged

Verbs contrast with non-factive verbs leave the proposition open: E.g.:

I believe he was overcharged

Reviewing the literature needs strategies to construct it. An important element is the reporting verbs. Reporting verbs are needed build up your phrases and paragraph "independently". There are common methods for writing a literature review section:

1. Paraphrasing
2. Quotation

Paraphrasing (إعادة الصياغة)

Paraphrasing is the process of re-writing the content of a passage (text) in a way different from the original form. This re-writing is to suit your style and purpose by expressing the meaning of a passage using your own vocabulary. Thesaurus or books of synonyms can provide you with useful alternative words and thus you avoid copyright and plagiarism or fraud. A good paraphrase must be:

1. Accurate
2. Original
3. Grammatically correct

The meaning of your paraphrased text must be the same as the source. However, the grammar and the wording may be different. For example:

"Ojo (1985) isolated *Mycobacterium senegalense* from cattle in Nigeria"

This can be paraphrased as follows:

"Cattle in Nigeria have been found to be infected with *Mycobacterium senegalense* (Ojo, 1985)"

You can join many sentences or shorten a long sentence by one or two verbs.

Words, which have no synonyms, remain the same. E.g.: Blood, potassium, gram, Europe etc.

 Try to adopt your own style of writing even if it does not look sparkling".

Quotation (اقتباس)

Quotation is the repeat of a statement. It is desired when the exact wording or statement of the original author is important or of interest.

In quotation, the followings should be noted:

1. Quotation should not be too much in your text
2. A quote must be absolutely accurate
3. A quote must be enclosed in a quotation marks

E.g.:

Pasteur (1900) said, "Where observation is concerned, chance favors only the prepared mind"

If the quote is long then it needs to be separated from the text by double lines or by aligning the quote 1-2 cm to the right or format the font in italics.etc...

A quote must be placed properly in your text and logically linked with the sequence of text by giving more linking words.

Examine the following examples:

"Mycolic acids are covalently linked to an arabinan unit of the wall arabinogalactan and hence various chemical treatments are required to release them. In early studies, alcoholic alkaline treatment was followed by estrification of the free acids with diazomethane. This procedure can cause racimization at C2 resulting in the formation of diaster co-isomers which occurs during thin layer chromatography (Minnikin and Polgar, 1966). Extracts were then esterified using a phase-transfer catalyzed procedure by dichoromethane and iodomethane (Dobson et al., 1985)."

In this example the author, avoid using reporting verbs excessively as seen in the first example. Here a simple story-like system was followed with references being rarely act as subject of the sentences. That is needed so as not to distract the reader's attention by excessive report of reference. Instead, few words were used to describe what has happened. In this example, the text is simple and direct, thus indicating the experience in writing.

Another example:

"Data on the extent of drug misuse among students, for example, vary and may be questionable. Surveys are based on self-reporting of a concealed activity such as the use of illegal drugs. In the Sudan, the available evidence suggests that the age of the first use of illegal drugs is 16-21 years old (Hakim, 1989; el Hilo, 1992). Evidently, the statistical records show an increase in numbers of young people who are seeking medical and physiological help for their drug related problems (El Tiganl El Mahi Psychiatric Hospital Official Record, 1985). Drugs misuse is an annoying issue for school in rural and urban areas. It extends across all socio-economic levels (UNISCO, 1995)."

DESIGN, METHODOLOGY AND PROCEDURES (PROTOCOL)

The following sections are normally included in the protocol:

1. Setting
2. Study design

3. Study population
4. Materials and equipments
5. Data collection (methods)
6. Data analysis (Statistics)

As with the theoretical framework and methodology, it is important to demonstrate that you have read other studies in your area of research. You should be able to address the strengths and limitations of the methods in similar research and justify why you have chosen the method that you have.

In your method, you should discuss the following aspects:

Setting

Setting includes the time, location, and everything in which a research takes place.

Study design

When choosing a study design (تصميم الدراسة), many factors must be taken into account. Different types of studies are subject to different types of bias (انحياز). Describe the type of study E.g.:

Observational studies, includes:

1. Cohort study (prospective cohort, retrospective cohort, time series study)
2. Case-control study (nested case-control study)
3. Cross-sectional study (community survey (a type of cross-sectional study)

Treatment studies can be:

1. Randomized controlled trial (double-blind randomized trial or single-blind randomized trial or non-blind trial)
2. Nonrandomized trial (quasi-experiment) it involves interrupted time series design (measures on a sample or a series of samples from the same population are obtained several times before and after a manipulated event or a naturally occurring event)

Study population

List number and groups of target populations and their relevant information.

(27)

Materials and equipments

List items needed for the research including equipment, instruments and consumables. These can be kits, chemicals, glassware, writing materials, safety items etc...

Data collection (methods)

How will you go about collecting your information (surveys, experiments, interviews)? This should also include any equipment or instruments that you will need for this purpose.

Methods

Strictly and accurately, describe methods you will follow or modified. Do not forget to cite the **original** reference from whom you copied the methods. Methods should not be attributed to the source from where you read it but to the original source in which it has been first described or first modified.

Example:

> Identification of yeasts encountered during routine bacteriological cultures or from SDA and BHIA plates was performed using conventional growth and colonial morphology criteria (Ellis, 2013.

Data analysis

Once you have the information, what will you do with it? Include any tools you will use to assist you with analysis (E.g.: Programs, Models). Indicate how would you analyze the data? In this way, you will answer your research question (s).

ETHICAL CONSIDERATIONS (WHERE APPLICABLE)

Statement of ethical clearance (الاعتبارات الأخلاقية) for the study can be placed here or separately (see below) or copy of it placed in the appendix.

Almost all research needs to consider ethics (الأخلاق). When appropriate, show readers that you have taken precautions to ensure that your research does not cause unnecessary harm to potential subjects participating in the study or to other individuals particularly humans or animal subjects. You should consider the rights of those being researched (including informed consent). It is your responsibility how data will be collected, stored or disposed of. You should indicate whether your proposal will require approval from an ethics committee and if so, which one? It is important that you familiarize yourself with ethical guidelines in your area such as taken permission or approval of the ministry or the governing body. E.g.: The study was approved by the National Ethic Committee, written consent was obtained from all patients before enrolment in the study.

DELIMITATION AND LIMITATION OF RESEARCH

Limitation factors are the ones that researcher has no control on such as" "the response of farmers" to the questionnaire and how correct his/her answers and statements. On the other hands, the delimitation factors are the ones which researcher has full control on. For example, the "level of organochlorine compound in farmer sample" is under his control because he/ she control the analysis, its quality process, and the resultant findings. Look at your methodology and consider any weaknesses or limitations that may occur because of your research design. Address the limitations by indicating how you will minimize them.

BIBLIOGRAPHY (REFERENCES)

A citation (استشهاد برأي، ذِكر) is the system by which you inform readers that some information in your manuscript (thesis/ paper/ book) is originated from another source. A bibliographic citation is the referencing to a published scientific material (book, article, web page, or other published items). Citation serves many purposes: to maintain the intellectual honesty and to avoid plagiarism. Moreover, it serves to accredit prior or unoriginal work and ideas to the correct sources and to allow readers to determine independently whether the referenced material supports the author's argument in the claimed way. In addition, it serves to help readers gauge measure the strength and validity of the material the author has used (ALWD, 2010).

There are two main systems for citing the references in thesis or in any other forms of writing:

1. Harvard system (Parenthetical)
2. British system (Vancouver)

Harvard system (Parenthetical)

Harvard system is also called the "Parenthetical referencing" uses the author's surname and the date of publication of the article or book in the text and then it lists alphabetically all the references in the reference list or bibliography, which usually comes last.

EXAMPLES OF CITATIONS IN THE HARVARD SYSTEM:

Psidium quajava K. (guava) is one of the most common fruits of the tropics. It originates in tropical America and has been distributed practically to all tropical and subtropical countries with substantial industries in India, Hawaii and South Africa (**Knight, 1980**). In India, guava ranks next to banana, mango and citrus in popularity (**Menzel and Paxton, 1986**).

Thortc and Chakrawar (1983) recognized the distribution and popularity of guava in all parts of India extending from north to equator. According to M. Imad of the department of horticulture, Khartoum (personal communication, 1990), the current major production areas are Kadaru, Gaili and Shendi, north of Khartoum. According to **Teotia et al. (1962**), the term of red-fleshed guavas covers the various shades of pink-fleshed fruits.

REFERENCES LIST OF THE ABOVE HARVARD SYSTEM:

Knight, R.Jr. (1980). Origin and world importance of tropical and subtropical fruit crops in: S. Nagy and P. S. Shaw (Eds.). Tropical and subtropical fruits: composition, properties and uses. AVI Publishing Incorporation, West Port, Conn. USA. Pp. 1-120.

Menzel, Z.M. and Paxton, B.F. (1986). The pattern of growth, flowering, fruiting of guava varieties in subtropical Queensland. Austr. J. Exp. Agric. 26: 43-48.

Teaotia, S.S. Panoky, I.C., Awasthi, R.K., Dobey, P.S. (1962). Further studies on guava (Poiduiro quajava L.). Punjab Hort. J. 9: 42-47.

Thortc, G.T. and Chakrawar, V.R. (1983). Studies on certain strains of guava fruits. J. Maharashtra agric. Univ. 8: 218-220.

British system (Vancouver)

The British system is also called "the Vancouver system" is a numeric one in which the reference cited in the text bears numbers: (1, 2, etc...) that are either positioned in brackets or as superscripts. The references appear in the text is then written in the reference list according to their numbers in text regardless of the alphabetical order (Neville, 2012).

EXAMPLES OF CITATIONS IN THE BRITISH SYSTEM:

Bracketed:

Psidium quajava L. (guava) is one of the most common fruits of the tropics. It originates in tropical America and has been distributed practically to all tropical and subtropical countries with substantial industries in India, Hawaii and South Africa (1). In India, guava ranks next to banana, mango and citrus in popularity (2).

Thortc and Chakrawar (3) recognized the distribution and popularity of guava in all parts of India extending from north to equator. According to M. Imad of the department of horticulture, Khartoum (personal communication, 1990), the current major production areas are Kadaru, Gaili and Shendi, north of Khartoum. According to Teotia et al. (4), the term of red-fleshed guavas covers the various shades of pink-fleshed fruits.

Alternatively, superscripted:

Psidium quajava L. (guava) is one of the most common fruits of the tropics. It originates in tropical America and has been distributed practically to all tropical and subtropical countries with substantial industries in India, Hawaii and South Africa. [1] In India, guava ranks next to banana, mango and citrus in popularity. [2]

Thortc and Chakrawar [3] recognized the distribution and popularity of guava in all parts of India extending from north to equator. According to M. Imad of the department of horticulture, Khartoum (personal communication, 1990), the current major production areas are Kadaru, Gaili and Shendi, north of Khartoum. According to Teotia et al. [4] the term of red-fleshed guavas covers the various shades of pink fleshed fruits.

REFERENCES LIST OF THE ABOVE CITATIONS IN THE BRITISH SYSTEM:

1. Knight, R.Jr. (1980). Origin and world importance of tropical and subtropical fruit crops in: S. Nagy and p. S. Shaw (Eds.). Tropical and subtropical fruits: composition, properties and uses. AVI Publishing, Inc., Westport, Connecticut, pp. 1-120.
2. Menzel, Z.M. and Paxton, B.F. (1986). The pattern of growth, flowering, fruiting of guava varieties in subtropical Queensland. Austr. J. Exp. Agric. 26: 43-48.
3. Thortc, G.T. and Chakrawar, V.R. (1983). Studies on certain strains of guava fruits. J. Maharashtra agric. Univ. 8: 218-220.
4. Teaotia, S.S. Panoky, I.C., Awasthi, R.K., Dobey, P.S. (1962). Further studies on guava (*Poiduiro quajava* L.). Punjab Hort. J. 9: 42-47.

Journals are abbreviated according to CAS (chemical abstracts service division of the American Chemical Society) or ISO (International Organization for Standardization) systems. E.g.:

— Advances in Chemical Physics, abbreviated as Adv. Chem. Phys.
— Current Molecular Medicine →Curr. Mol. Med.
— Bulletin of Materials Science → Bull. Mater. Sci.

- Water Resources → Water Resour.

DEFINITION OF TERMINOLOGY

Definition of terminology is important, because some concepts/ terms are often used in different meanings by different authors. E.g.: Culture in biological science means to cultivate/ isolate microorganisms in artificial media; media (sing. medium) is a vehicle containing nutrients to support the growth of microorganisms. Whereas, culture in humanities means civilization, society, tradition or customs or the sum of all these, and media in humanities means information (news) device.

TIME SCHEDULE

A timeline that estimates how long each task will take helps determine the scope of your research and if it is achievable within a given timeframe. Your research proposal timeline should include time allocation for a detailed E.g.:

Task	Months	From	To
Literature review	....	....	....
Time for approval from ethics committee	....	....	....
Reviewing or testing of research design	....	....	....
Data collection	....	....	....
Data analysis	....	....	....
Writing up of findings	....	....	....
Etc...	....	....	....

It is important to be realistic with the timeframe, consider if you are able to dedicate full time work to the research, of if it is to be conducted while you are studying other papers, working part or full time or have family commitments.
Budget

Upon request, funding for research (a budget) is included to indicate where funds will be allocated. A summary of budget may include items such as:

Items	Cost (currency)
Survey design	....
Consumables and equipments	....
Research assistants	....
Printing	....
Software	....
Etc...	....
Total	....

Another example:

	Year 1	Year 2	Year 3	Total
Personnel	......	......	......	......
Principal investigator	......	......	......	......
Research assistant	......	......	......	......
Staff	......	......	......	......
Tuition/fees	......	......	......	......
Subtotal personnel	......	......	......	......
Project expenses	......	......	......	......
Fees/stipends	......	......	......	......
Supplies	......	......	......	......
Communication	......	......	......	......
Transcription	......	......	......	......
Equipment	......	......	......	......
Travel	......	......	......	......
Miscellaneous	......	......	......	......
Subtotal project exp.	......	......	......	......
Total direct costs	......	......	......	......
Indirect costs (15%)	......	......	......	......
Total project costs	......	......	......	......

APPENDIX

Some useful appendix (ملحق) includes:

Data gathering instruments, i.e. Questionnaire forms, interview schedule, etc.

Timeline of research process (a table)

Consent forms

Draft surveys/questionnaires

Section 3: **THESIS**

OBJECTIVES OF THESIS

Objectives of thesis differ with the degree intended and with points of view of researchers, advisors and those who will read it. Three major objectives are widely accepted and popular, they constitute the major points that may lead separately or collectively to solving the identified problem (Fig. 1).

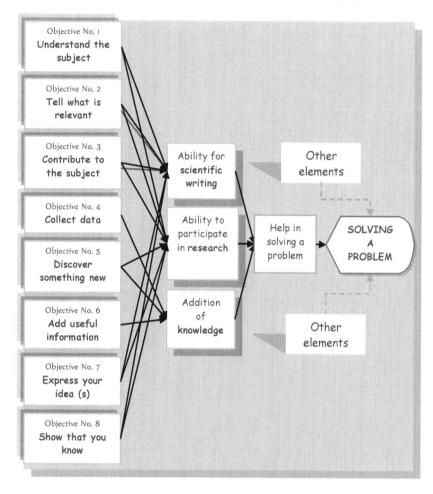

Figure 1: *A chart showing the integrated objectives of a thesis (research)*

MAJOR OBJECTIVES

1. To add knowledge

   To add to the body of knowledge necessary information to solve problem facing the profession or rather helps solving the problem under study.

2. To be able to write

   To establish student ability to write about professional and scientific data in an understandable way to people who need such information.

3. To be able to participate in research

   One of the major aims is to prepare student for participation in research as part of his/ her career in the profession.

MINOR OBJECTIVES

Minor objectives that lead to the above three (or one) major objective (s) include:

1. understand your subject
2. to tell what is relevant
3. collect new data
4. contribute to your subject
5. discover something new
6. to show how much you know
7. to express your own ideas

TYPE OF THESIS AND METHODS OF INVESTIGATION

Many types of scientific investigations are being undertaken by researcher to produce a thesis or dissertation to fulfill the requirements for obtaining a higher degree.

Shaw (1991) considered that any action that leads to accurate statement about nature must be considered as having some methodological legitimacy. Humanity learned much about human nature long before there was a formal recognition of science and scientific methods.

The following 14 types of research (Mauch and Birch, 1990) are commonly practiced, each suits a particular problem, and one on more types may be followed for certain research. The type of research adopted will affect the produced thesis or dissertation and it is acceptable to be named according to the type of research, e.g.: Analytical, comparative, developmental or case study... Etc.

ANALYTICAL

Classes of data are collected and studies are conducted to detect and explain principles, which might guide action.

Examples:

- State court interpretations of permissive legislation on non- school use of school property criteria for accepting applicants in housing
- Co-operatives epidemiology of juvenile diabetes mellitus management of extremes of human behavior in hospital emergency rooms
- Employment of handicapped high- school graduates an economically depressed region

COMPARATIVE

Two or more existing situations are studied in order to determine and clarify their likeness and differences.

Examples:

- Concepts taught in secondary school chemistry in Canada, Great Britain, New Zealand, and the United States
- Self-control of children and adults during cardiac diagnostic procedures
- Bid specification procedures for public playground and recreation supply and equipment purchases in New York, Pennsylvania, Illinois, and California
- Government and volunteer agency behavior in times of crisis

CORRELATION-PREDICTIVE

Statistically significant correlation coefficients between and among relevant phenomena are sought and interpret; this type includes the determination of the extent to which variations in one or more factors correspond with variations in one or more other factors and the use of such findings in making predictions.

Examples:

- Alteration of gasoline prices and automobile travel for business and vacation purposes
- Relationship of vocational success and social and emotional problems among nurses
- Relationships between nature of crime and amount of recidivism relations among size of family, age, and use of home health agencies relationship between teacher backgrounds and their attitudes toward international co-operation.

DESIGN AND DEMONSTRATION

New operationally related business systems, personnel training curricula, professional education programs, instructional materials, disease control plans, and the like are constructed and described; this type is often called action research and includes, at least, formative evaluation.

Examples:

- A literacy program for the Sudan
- A cytotoxicity test for insoluble dusts
- Design and establishment of a comprehensive health information system for Western Australia.

DEVELOPMENTAL

The changes over time in one or more observable factors, patterns, or sequences of growth or decline may be traced or charted and reported.

Examples:

- Growth of child care centers in American business and industry
- State control of public secondary school curriculum from 1900 to 1975
- Emergence and spread of credit card utilization
- The written language development of children
- The computer and the knowledge explosion: a developmental study

EXPERIMENTAL

One or more variables may be deliberately manipulated and the results analyzed and rationalized- "true" experiments requiring tight controls and subject randomization.

Examples:

- Reduction of separation anxiety through use of mental imagery
- Use of programmed instruction to correct errors in the written language of deaf adolescents
- The effects of listening training on salesperson effectiveness
- Effects of a parental intervention strategy on reading skill development
- Effects of different options for continued employment on retirement decisions

HISTORICAL

Individuals or activities are studied to reconstruct the past accurately and without bias in order to discover, document, and interpret their influences or to check the tenability of a hypothesis.

Examples:

- The relevance of the thought of Albert Camus for education
- Sources of individual differences in solutions to management problems
- Historical landmarks in the management of environmental noise
- The search for the perpetual motion machine: its contribution to engineering
- Origins and status of the Montessori movement in the United States

OPINION POLLING

The behaviors, beliefs, or intentions of specified groups of persons are determined, reported, and interpreted.

Examples:

- Food preferences of hospitalized individuals by age and geographical region in Canada
- Opinions of students and alumni regarding the graduate program in counseling psychology
- Political and social beliefs of experienced engineers
- Citizen views on a volunteer system of armed forces
- Attitudes of Sunday school teachers toward religious and secular educational objectives

STATUS

A representative or selected sample of one or more phenomena may be isolated and examined in order to ascertain the characteristics of the object (s) of study.

Examples:

- Freemasonry in New Zealand: contemporary status
- The mail order catalogue business in America
- The training, background, duties, activities, and job perceptions of public health officers
- Employment among minorities in large U.S. cities
- The yearbook in public high schools

THEORETICAL

Complete and economical explanatory principles for phenomena or data are developed, proposed, and described.

Examples:

- A conceptual analysis of creativity
- A theory of compensatory education
- An explanatory model for mass appraisal: extension of Rosen's theory of implicit markets to urban housing
- A psychological theory to explain faith healing
- A theory of intellectual evolution

TREND ANALYSIS

Phenomena that are or have been in the process of change are examined in order to identify and report the directions of trends and to make interpretations and forecasts.

Examples:

- Trends in the teaching of parenting in American secondary schools
- The use of public transportation in Mexico: a trend analysis
- Dow-Jones average changes during selected periods of federal monetary policy
- Trends in availability and cost of dental health insurance
- Trends in public tax support for private colleges and universities

CASE STUDY

The background, development, current condition, and environmental interactions of one or more individuals, groups, communities businesses or institutions are observed, recorded.

Examples:

- A case study of open admissions in an American junior college
- The development of cognitive functions in three autistic children: case records analyses
- Establishment and growth of the national association of retired persons
- The origin and development of the intermediate unit as a service delivery agency in public education
- The national association of manufacturers' labors policy: a case study of development

QUASI-EXPERIMENTAL

In quasi-experimental (شبه تجریبیة) a rigor experiments as manipulation, control, or randomization is not feasible but the comparison of treatment versus non-treatment conditions is approximated and the compromises and limitations are stated, understood, and taken into account in all conclusions and interpretations.

(41)

Examples:

All of the examples under item (Experimental) would be applicable here if they were carried out under conditions in which only partial control was possible of variables, treatments, populations, or other important conditions. The case in many real-life situations where filed. Operational studies are the only feasible kinds if professional and ethical codes are to be properly upheld.

EVALUATION

A program or a project is expected to be carried out in a certain way and expected to produce a certain result; research is intended to determine whether the anticipated procedure and the out-come are realized; evaluation research that focuses on the procedure is called summative.

Examples:

- Effectiveness of mental health programs on impaired children
- Evaluation of a regional family planning programs
- Impact of county drug and alcohol programs
- Evaluation of a rural marketing plan for fire insurance
- Effectiveness of rehabilitation counseling: an evaluation

STAGES AND TIMETABLE OF A THESIS

A completed thesis generally undergoes a chronology (Fig. 2), which start after the approval of the proposal, therefore, use proposal to execute thesis.

1.	→	Investigate the identified problem Do practical part and collect data as described in proposal (perform experiments, test target population, extract, isolate treat etc). This is the first thing you do after approving proposal.	→	Write this part to from **Materials and methods**
2.	→	Data collection and analysis Record and analyze data, with or without graphics, tables... Etc. (as described in proposal)	→	Write this part to from **Results**
3.	→	Criticize, relate ad argue the recorded data	→	Write this part to from **Discussion**
4.	→	Convey conclusions and implications to others	→	Write this part to from **Conclusions and recommendations**
5.	→	Write and arrange thesis into chapters: title page, summary, introduction, literature review, methods, results, discussion, conclusions, references, and appendix.	→	**1st Draft**
6.	→	It is essential that thesis writer checks (proof read) his/her text for common errors E.g.: Punctuations, omissions, spellings, agreement, singular/ plural, headings, verbs...	→	**Proof-reading**
7.	→	One of the requirements for certain advanced degrees is often an oral examination or a presentation by the student and questions by an examining committee or jury	→	**Thesis Defense** (viva voce)
8.	→	The student must submit a complete copy of the thesis to institution, along with the appropriate completed forms	→	**Submission**

FIGURE 2: *STAGES AND TIMETABLE OF A THESIS*

Structure (Anatomy) of the Thesis

A finished thesis differs from the written proposal but some sections look similar except that the thesis is written in the past tenses whereas the proposal is written in future tenses.

There are general guidelines for thesis writing (see below). Students should check with institution guidelines for local rules and variations. Examples of a variation of theses is taken from Lindsay (1989) and shown in Table 2.

A typical thesis consists of major sections with some variations (see below) which can be noticed between different thesis systems:

1. Title page
2. Dedication (if there is any)
3. Table of contents (Index)
4. Acknowledgement (s)
5. Summary (abstract)
6. Introduction and objectives
7. Chapter 1: Literature Review
8. Chapter 2: Materials and Methods
9. Results
10. Discussion and conclusions
11. References
12. Appendix (if there is any)

Three models for a thesis construction are generally accepted:

Model A (Lindsay, 1989)	Model B	Model C
– Title page	– Title page	– Title page
– Summary (abstract)	– Summary (abstract)	– Summary (abstract)
– General introduction	– Introduction	– Introduction and review of the literature
– Review of the literature	– Review of the literature	
– General materials and methods	– Materials and methods	– Materials and methods
– Experiments chapters	– Results	– Results
– General discussion	– Discussion	– Discussion
– Bibliography	– Bibliography	– Bibliography

In addition to the main sections shown up, there are small sections namely: acknowledgements, Table of Contents or index (including lists of tables and figures, statutory declaration, dedications, appendices and other materials demanded by the institution or supervisor according to studies. The model approved in this book is detailed down.

TITLE PAGE

It includes:

1. Name of university/ institution
2. Title of the thesis
3. Name and qualifications of candidate
4. Name and qualifications of advisors/ supervisors with or without their undertaken (signatures)
5. Date of submission

DEDICATION (IF THERE IS ANY)

Some students would like to dedicate (يهدي) the thesis for someone special E.g.: This thesis is dedicated to my father ....; Dr .... who .... etc...

ACKNOWLEDGEMENTS

It is strongly recommended that students acknowledge (يعترف، يعبر عن شكره) those who help him/her during his/ her research including institutions, company and individuals. E.g.: "I would like to thank my supervisor, Mr. _____, for the valuable advice and support he has given me in the writing of this report. I would also like to thank my teachers, Mrs. _____ and Mr. _____ for their encouragement and guidance. Thanks also to my typist, Mrs. _____, for her immaculate job and her suggestions. My deepest thanks go to my wife/husband, for her/his love, understanding and support."

SUMMARY (ABSTRACT)

The summary (abstract: الملخص) has the same purpose and same form as the summary for a scientific article. It should be factual and comprehensive containing the fundamental nature of all sections of the research project. It usually contains (structured format):

1. Re-statement of the general hypothesis and aims
2. Design, setting and overall procedure for the research
3. The main results and their significance

4. General conclusion, main outcome, measures and interpretation

It is usually does not include references and graphics.

Summaries of five to six pages are no longer summaries. Therefore, if results are large, trimming should be adopted to fit it into a "summary". Describe the principle results, which lead you to make the conclusion. In the final part of the summary, list the main conclusions, which you discuss in the discussion chapter.

E.g.:

- This study was to _____
- The investigation was done by _____
- The main findings were that _____
- It was concluded that _____
- The recommendations are that _____should be

INTRODUCTION AND OBJECTIVES

This section does not differ from that written for the proposal (section 2). The purpose of this section is to provide a background for the material to follow and to set up the hypothesis and to state the objectives.

The following elements are usually discussed in the introduction:

1. Statement of the problem
2. Research question (s)
3. Hypothesis
4. Significant and research outcomes
5. Objectives

STATEMENT OF THE PROBLEM (THEME)

Research forms a circle, it starts with a problem and ends with a solution to the problem. This is a summary of research theme, aims and objectives and it indicates the originality of your research or gabs, which your research will fill. The statement give direction to the study, it gives information about the scope and suggested how the study will be done. The statement, after all, must be clear concise and unambiguous. The research problem should be stated in such a way that it would lead to analytical thinking on the part of the researcher with the aim of possibly concluding solutions to the stated problem.

Examples:

"This thesis deals with cotton marketing and manufacturing in the Sudan (Zulfo, 1981)

"This study concerns with the prevention of drug misuse among secondary school students in Khartoum state" (El Hilo, 1992)

The purpose of this study is to investigate creativity among children in selected school in Khartoum state with emphasis on the use of drawing as an indicator

The increase use of organochlorine insecticide in the irrigated schemes dictates the importance of investigating the hazardous effects of these compounds on human and animal. This study is an attempt to detect organochlorine residues in samples from farmers and to correlate the presence of these residues with the occurrence of the lung cancer among farmer

Elements (below in bold) and objectives (to ...) extracted from the above statement can be written as direct objective as follows:

1. To detect **residues** of organochlorine insecticide in farmers samples
2. To record clinical and **pathological findings** in the tested farmers
3. To **correlate** between the level of organochlorine compounds in farmers samples and the recorded clinical signs

RESEARCH QUESTIONS

Examples of research questions:

1. Why there are more lung cancer cases among farmers than other sectors of the community?
2. Is there any relation between the level of organochlorine compounds in farmer's samples and the occurrence of lung cancer among farmers?
3. How can the secondary school students in Asir province be helped before the time when they will be forced by a series of decisions about drug?

HYPOTHESIS

To turn the research question: why there is more lung cancer among farmers than other sectors of the community? Into hypothesis as follows:

"frequent application of the organochlorine insecticide in farms resulted in the development of lung cancer among farmers".

How to build up a hypothesis was detailed earlier in section 2.

Example:

"Ultra violet light may cause skin cancer" this can be formalized as follows: "if skin cancer is related to ultraviolet light, then people with a high exposure to UV light will have a higher frequency of skin cancer"

"Plant growth may be affected by the color of the light" this can be formalized as follows: "if leaf color change is related to temperature, then exposing plants to low temperatures will result in changes in leaf color"

"The failure of pregnancy in sheep in the "x "region is due to the high temperature". This hypothesis was constructed because the student has some knowledge. Examples of his knowledge or facts:

SIGNIFICANT AND RESEARCH OUTCOMES

The researcher should indicate and defend why it is necessary to undertake the research. The benefits that will result from the research and to whom it will be beneficial should be indicated. You need to communicate enthusiasm and confidence for the research, arguing clearly as to the contribution it will make to the subject area and discipline in general the significance of the study is another way of starting the aims of the study.

Examples:

- Early targeted prevention programs in drug use among people can reduce long-term costs in the general medical sector. It also enhances the overall efficiency of health care service delivery
- Participation (objectively) in deterring and eradication of drug miscue emphasize prevention of problems that affect security of society such as cultivation of Hashish
- The study call for further research
- The study provides a comprehensive analysis
- There is wide availability and cultivation of Hashish, therefore, there is need for highlighting the fact of the availability
- There is a fact that: secondary school students are "misuses of drugs": fact from current knowledge and hence it state the need for something to done i.e. Significance of the study

OBJECTIVES

THE GENERAL OBJECTIVE

You can state the general objective in a statement as follows:

The objective of this study is to assess the nature and extent of drug misuse among secondary school in Khartoum province and to provide information, which might help in preventing drug misuse among secondary school student in the province.

MEASURABLE (SPECIFIC) OBJECTIVES

To acquire knowledge about drug to understand its devastating effect, its low and legislation

To stimulate more negative attitude towards drug use

To develop a sense of moral and values to raise the level of their self-esteem.

To improve of their decision making skill and enable them to avoid the misuse of drug

CHAPTER 1: LITERATURE REVIEW

The literature review for thesis does not differ from that written for the proposal, only that here more details are given and student expected to survey almost all information published and relevant on his/ her subject. Go back to section 2 (reviewing the literature) and follow the description of literature review: aims, methods and examples.

CHAPTER 2: MATERIALS AND METHODS

In methods researcher describe sampling procedure, design, equipments, methods of study, statistical analysis in sufficient details to allow reproduction by other workers.

The purpose of the materials and methods is to describe completely how each experiment was done. Repeating similar techniques for each experiment would be time consuming, boring and distracting. Therefore, it is common to include a chapter, which gathers together the techniques used in most of the experiments. This has two advantages: it avoid repetition and it clear it clear and it clears the way for results of related experiments to be presented uninterrupted by long tracts of methodology.

It is importance to mention the valid method used. Otherwise, some methods may need small test (pilot) experiments.

Experimental procedure are often substituted for "materials and methods" to avoid confusion.

CHAPTER 3: RESULTS

Present results in logic sequence. Avoid repetition between text and illustrations. Numbers should match with all sections of the thesis (paper). Use uniform unit of measurement.

Results can be written with subtitles commonly the match those written in methodology chapter. E.g.: If in method there is survey (how, when and where) then in results there should be a survey subtitle to list the results of that survey.

Use text to explain supported by tables and figures (if there is any) examples:

Out of the 1000 sputum samples cultivated, growth of mycobacterium tuberculosis in LJ media was obtained in 552 (55.2%), the results are shown in table 1.

When using primer tb40 and tb41 to amplify the specific m. Tuberculosis is6110 sequences in sputum samples, 46 were found positive on gel electrophoresis (Fig. 11).

The clinical results of the treatment trials for the five groups were as follows: group 1 (control): no change in the clinical picture was noticed in three... Etc.

CHAPTER 4: DISCUSSION, CONCLUSIONS AND RECOMMENDATIONS

DISCUSSION

Discussion is the only chapter in which the writer can express his/ her ideas or criticize other works based on his/ her findings and not on any other ground. It provides implications and interpretations of findings, their major breakthrough and or limitations. It relates observations to relevant study and present status of knowledge.

In discussion, do not repeat data from introduction or findings from the results section unless warranted. Discussion meant to focus on important finding to project them, to support them to make them important and significant or to show their advantage or otherwise (fair criticism), to give them their true value, to show shortage of the results, deficiency or any disadvantages.

Do not just criticize based on your own results, you have to use other similar (relevant) published results, make comparisons show which one is better and why avoid bias in terms of selecting certain papers and neglecting other because they do not agree with yours. Indicate why this result is important and on the other hand indicate why this result is insignificant or unimportant and list reason for that poorness or lack of goodness of the results and most importantly give ideas about how in future to correct these defects.

E.g.:

The present results confirm and extend those from previous studies (Trujillo and Goodfellow 2003; Quintana et al. 2008) as the strains isolated from biopsy material taken from mycetoma patients in the Sudan fell into several well delineated centers of taxonomic variation in the genus *Streptomyces* etc.

In the present study calcium level improves significantly after treatment (p = 0.021). This result approved those of Kapu (11) who observed decreased in calcium levels among infected animals etc...

CONCLUSIONS

Sum up the main findings and their interpretation affirming clearly the message of the paper.

E.g.:

(51)

- The main conclusion that can be drawn is, therefore, that...
- In the light of this, it is recommended that...

The detailed recommendations should go in the recommendations section below.

The present study concluded that: *Escherichia coli* accounts for 57.2% of community-acquired urinary tract infections diagnosed in Aseer region. The resistance rate of uropathogenic *E. coli* to trimethoprim-sulfamethoxazole (TMP-SMX) was found very high (49.8%).

RECOMMENDATIONS

In this section, you indicate for future research:

- The problems (objectives) that needed to be achieved (solved) from where you have stopped. E.g.:, the present study recommends for future research and clinical applications the following:
- Continued surveillance of resistance rates among uropathogens is needed to ensure appropriate recommendations for the empiric therapy for urinary tract infections
- Reassessment of local empiric choices for managing catheter-associated urinary tract infections is continuously needed due to evolving change in drug resistance
- In the light of these conclusions, I recommend that _____ should be _____. In addition, a _____ could _____

BIBLIOGRAPHY (REFERENCES)

A citation (ذِكر، برأي استشهاد) is the system by which you inform readers that some information in your manuscript (thesis/ paper/ book) is originated from another source. A bibliographic citation is the referencing to a published scientific material (book, article, web page, or other published items). Citation serves many purposes: to maintain the intellectual honesty and to avoid plagiarism. Moreover, it serves to accredit prior or unoriginal work and ideas to the correct sources and to allow readers to determine independently whether the referenced material supports the author's argument in the claimed way. In addition, it serves to help readers gauge measure the strength and validity of the material the author has used (ALWD, 2010).

There are two main systems for citing the references in thesis or in any other forms of writing:

3. Harvard system (Parenthetical)
4. British system (Vancouver)

Harvard system (Parenthetical)

Harvard system is also called the "Parenthetical referencing" uses the author's surname and the date of publication of the article or book in the text and then it lists alphabetically all the references in the reference list or bibliography, which usually comes last.

EXAMPLES OF CITATIONS IN THE HARVARD SYSTEM:

Psidium quajava K. (guava) is one of the most common fruits of the tropics. It originates in tropical America and has been distributed practically to all tropical and subtropical countries with substantial industries in India, Hawaii and South Africa (**Knight, 1980**). In India, guava ranks next to banana, mango and citrus in popularity (**Menzel and Paxton, 1986**).

Thortc and Chakrawar (1983) recognized the distribution and popularity of guava in all parts of India extending from north to equator. According to M. Imad of the department of horticulture, Khartoum (personal communication, 1990), the current major production areas are Kadaru, Gaili and Shendi, north of Khartoum. According to **Teotia et al. (1962)**, the term of red-fleshed guavas covers the various shades of pink-fleshed fruits.

REFERENCES LIST OF THE ABOVE HARVARD SYSTEM:

Knight,. (1980). Origin and world importance of tropical and subtropical fruit crops in: S. Nagy and P. S. Shaw (Eds.). Tropical and subtropical fruits: composition, properties and uses. AVI Publishing Incorporation, West Port, Conn. USA. Pp. 1-120.

Menzel, Z.M. And Paxton, B.F. (1986). The pattern of growth, flowering, fruiting of guava varieties in subtropical Queensland. Austr. J. Exp. Agric. 26: 43-48.

Teaotia, S.S. Panoky, I.C., Awasthi, R.K., Dobey, P.S. (1962). Further studies on guava (*Poiduiro quajava* L.). Punjab Hort. J. 9: 42-47.

Thortc, G.T. and Chakrawar, V.R. (1983). Studies on certain strains of guava fruits. J. Maharashtra agric. Univ. 8: 218-220.

The British system is also called "the Vancouver system" is a numeric one in which the reference cited in the text bears numbers: (1, 2, etc...) that are either positioned in brackets or as superscripts. The references appear in the text is then written in the reference list according to their numbers in text regardless of the alphabetical order (Neville, 2012).

EXAMPLES OF CITATIONS IN THE BRITISH SYSTEM:

Bracketed:

Psidium quajava L. (guava) is one of the most common fruits of the tropics. It originates in tropical America and has been distributed practically to all tropical and subtropical countries with substantial industries in India, Hawaii and South Africa (1). In India, guava ranks next to banana, mango and citrus in popularity (2).

Thortc and Chakrawar (3) recognized the distribution and popularity of guava in all parts of India extending from north to equator. According to M. Imad of the department of horticulture, Khartoum (personal communication, 1990), the current major production areas are Kadaru, Gaili and Shendi, north of Khartoum. According to Teotia et al. (4), the term of red-fleshed guavas covers the various shades of pink-fleshed fruits.

Alternatively, superscripted:

Psidium quajava L. (guava) is one of the most common fruits of the tropics. It originates in tropical America and has been distributed practically to all tropical and subtropical countries with substantial industries in India, Hawaii and South Africa. [1] In India, guava ranks next to banana, mango and citrus in popularity. [2]

Thortc and Chakrawar [3] recognized the distribution and popularity of guava in all parts of India extending from north to equator. According to M. Imad of the department of horticulture, Khartoum (personal communication, 1990), the current major production areas are Kadaru, Gaili and Shendi, north of Khartoum. According to Teotia et al. [4], the term of red-fleshed guavas covers the various shades of pink-fleshed fruits.

REFERENCES LIST OF THE ABOVE CITATIONS IN THE BRITISH SYSTEM:

5. Knight,. (1980). Origin and world importance of tropical and subtropical fruit crops in: S. Nagy and p. S. Shaw (Eds.). Tropical and subtropical fruits: composition, properties and uses. AVI Publishing, Inc., Westport, Connecticut, pp. 1-120.

6. Menzel, Z.M. and Paxton, B.F. (1986). The pattern of growth, flowering, fruiting of guava varieties in subtropical Queensland. Austr. J. Exp. Agric. 26: 43-48.
7. Thortc, G.T. and Chakrawar, V.R. (1983). Studies on certain strains of guava fruits. J. Maharashtra agric. Univ. 8: 218-220.
8. Teaotia, S.S. Panoky, I.C., Awasthi, R.K., Dobey, P.S. (1962). Further studies on guava (*Poiduiro quajava* L.). Punjab Hort. J. 9: 42-47.

Journals are abbreviated according to CAS (chemical abstracts service division of the American Chemical Society) or ISO (International Organization for Standardization) systems. E.g.:

- Advances in Chemical Physics, abbreviated as Adv. Chem. Phys.
- Current Molecular Medicine →Curr. Mol. Med.
- Bulletin of Materials Science → Bull. Mater. Sci.
- Water Resources → Water Resour.

APPENDIX (IF THERE ANY)

Some useful appendix includes:

1. Data gathering instruments, i.e. Questionnaire forms, interview schedule, etc.
2. Timeline of research process (a table)
3. Consent forms
4. Draft surveys/questionnaires

E.g.:

Appendix 1: sample survey form

Appendix 2: results of statistical analysis by _____

PROOF- READING

It is essential that thesis writer checks (proof read; تصحيح التجارب المطبعية) his/her text for common errors. Improvement of text can develop rapidly if the checking process is done carefully from the first draft. Check the first or the second draft before you hand it over to your advisor or a friend and similarly you check your final copy before you submit it to the higher institution. Errors and even mistakes are there is your text but the common believes that "it is all right from your point of view".

Minimizing the common errors (the silly one) from your draft text give your advisor the opportunity to implement constructive amendments rather than divert (occupy) his/her attention into these simple errors. Careful proof reading produces a final copy with little or no errors. Such a copy creates a positive impression on the examiners (readers).

The following point has been adapted from show (1991) and writers need to pay careful attention to the followings:

SPELLING

In particular, look for typing errors and missing double letters

(Alternatively, use the spellchecker on your PC or word processor).

PUNCTUATION

- Have you used capital letters at the beginning of sentences, etc?

- Have you used full stops not commas between sentences?

VERBS

- Does every sentence have a main verb?

- Do you know what tense each verb is in and why?

AGREEMENT

- Do the verbs agree with their subjects?

- Do words like this/these and that/those agree with the nouns they modify?

- Do pronouns like it and they agree with the nouns they refer to?

SINGULAR AND PLURAL

- Have you used nouns like equipment or research correctly as uncountable?

- Have you used countable nouns correctly in the singular or plural?

- Does an article precede all singular countable nouns?

SENTENCES

- *Are there any very long sentences that should be divided?*

OMISSIONS

- Have you accidentally left any words out?

HEADINGS

— Have you used capitals, underlining, and numbering consistently?

OTHERS REQUIREMENTS

Presentation requirements including pagination, layout, type and color of paper, use of acid-free paper (where a copy of the dissertation will become a permanent part of the library collection), paper size, order of components, and citation style, will be checked page by page by the accepting office.

STUDENT-SUPERVISOR RELATIONSHIP

Student-supervisor relationship is mostly an academic one. Nevertheless, it always moves on beyond that to a significantly productive and durable one. The process of constructing a successful thesis is certainly based on mutual trust and respect.

Shaw (1991) considers a positive student is the one from whom the supervisor/ advisor expects the followings:

1. Compatibility to accepted methodology and conventions
2. Independent initiative
3. New ideas
4. A statement of your needs
5. Well-presented written work at regular
6. Efforts to contact and get advice from other exports
7. Regular meetings (at least monthly)
8. Help with his/her research
9. Joint authorship of your publications
10. Lists of what you have read and plan to read
11. Honest reports of your progress
12. Information about your problems
13. Acceptance of their advice
14. Interest in your own work
15. Surprising information they did not know
16. A serious approach to your research
17. A good personal relationship
18. Patience in waiting until he/she is available
19. Attendance to his/her lectures
20. Information in new developments in the field

On the other hand, Shaw (1991) expects the followings from student to generate a good and creative research and thesis:

1. Intellectual stimulation
2. Weekly meetings
3. Psychological support
4. Guidance to the literature
5. Training in research methods
6. Evaluation of other's work
7. Explanation of the literature
8. Provision of a research design
9. Provision of a suitable topic
10. Friendship
11. Feedback on your ideas
12. Help with his/her experience of research
13. Criticism of work which is below standards
14. Correction of your English
15. A plan (structure) for your dissertation
16. A timetable for your research
17. Help in focusing the topic
18. Advice on personal difficulties
19. Opportunities to meet other people interested in your field
20. Proof-reading of your thesis
21. Feedback on the content of what you have written
22. Feedback on the organization of what have your written

FURTHER READINGS

Association of Legal Writing Directors & Darby Dickerson, ALWD (2010) *Citation Manual: A Professional System of Citation*, 4th ed., New York: Aspen

Bell J (1987) *Doing Your Research Paper.* Milton Keynes, Open University press

Coper BM (1984) *Writing Technical Reports.* Harmondsworth, Penguin

El Hilo B (1992) PhD Thesis, University of Khartoum

Hamp-lyons L and Courter KB (1984) *Research Matters.* Cambridge MA. Newbury House

Hart C (2001) *Doing A Literature Search. A Comprehensive Guide for the Social Sciences.* London: Sage

How to do a literature review? (Quoted 2010) North Carolina A & T State University. http://www.library.ncat.edu/ref/guides/literaturereview

International standard ISO 7144: *Documentation- Presentation of Theses and Similar Documents.* International Organization for Standardization, Geneva, 1986

Lindsay D (1989) *A Guide to Scientific Writing.* Longman Cheshire

Mackernan J (1991). *The Writers Handbook.* Holt Rinehart, Webster

Mauch JE and Birch JW (1990) *Guide to the successful thesis: conception to publication: a handbook for students and faculty.* 2nd ed. Marcel Dekker, Inc. New York

Multimedia Publishing (1975) Report writing, London.

Neville C (2012) Referencing: Principles, practices and problems. In *RGUHS Journal of Pharmaceutical Sciences*, 2: 1-8

Phillips EM and Pugh DS (1987) *How to Get a PhD?* Milton Keynes, Open University Press

Shaw P (1991) A Course in Writing Dissertation and Theses. The Language Centre, University of Newcastle

Stuart EB (1979) A Manual for Preparation of Theses and Dissertations. Fourth Ed.). Pittsburgh, PA: The University of Pittsburgh

Tape-Slide Presentation (1991) obtainable form undergraduate reference collection, Main Library, University of Newcastle

INDEX

Printed in Great Britain
by Amazon